Violet Flame
— and Other —
Meditations

By Gillian DeArmond

· ·

AMERICA WEST
PUBLISHERS

JOANNE HEINZ
P.O. Box 411
Ravenna, Ohio   44266

Library of Congress Cataloging-in-Publication Data

DeArmond, Gillian, 1937-
    Violet Flame and Other Meditations / by Gillian DeArmond.
    p. cm.
    ISBN 0-922356-19-X : $5.95
    1. Meditation. 2. New Age Movement. I. Title.
BP605.N48D42 1990   90-33822
131--dc20   CIP

First Edition Printed by America West Publishers, 1990

Cover Design: Alicia Nieboer

Published by
AMERICA WEST PUBLISHERS
P.O. Box 6451
Tehachapi, CA 93582

Printed in the United States of America

10 9 8 7 6 5 4 3 2 1

CONTENTS

• • • • • • • • • • • • • • • • • • •

List of Figures

●●●●●●●●●●●●●●●●●●●●

A Message from the Author

Dear Friends,

The foundation of all that I teach is given to me by the spiritual Teacher, David, and directly channeled to me. May I stress that at no time do I go into a trance or otherwise allow the teaching guides to control my mind or body. The need to always stay in control of oneself was impressed upon me most strongly during the years when I was learning to discipline myself for clairvoyant work. It took many more years to reach the desired level of clarity by staying in control than if I had simply allowed myself to be "taken over" as a channel. Although I accepted this discipline without question at the time, more recently I have asked for an explanation of the reasoning behind my training. The response I was given was; "any entity 'taking over' the will control of another living being is breaking the first rule of the universe, namely, the rule of non- interference with the lifestream of another, and only those entities working from the astral plane and still attached to the planet by their ego would wish to do this. While we do not say that there is not some good teaching for the planet from this (the astral) level, we do repeat that no entity evolved beyond the astral level would wish to act in this way but would rather wait until the chosen vessel is able to receive their guidance in the fully aware state".

As with all I am given to teach, it is for *YOU* to decide the value of the lesson.

Truly, in Light,
Gillian

◢1◣ STANDARD MEDITATION PROCEDURES.

There is an expression which says " Prayer is asking questions and meditation is receiving answers". In order to hear the answers you must *be quiet* and *be aware*; that is the state of meditation. This first chapter tells you how to go into the meditation state and is referred to throughout these pages as your "standard meditation technique".

When beginning the practice of meditation the first thing to consider is location; In what environment will you meditate best? Choose a location which will be readily available to you on a regular basis, that's the first step. Next, make sure that when you want to meditate you will not be disturbed No phone calls, door bells, clothes dryers or visitors interrupting you, in fact, no distractions of any kind. For many of you this may mean rising early in the morning or waiting until the rest of the household has retired at night. Having chosen a suitable location your next step is to make sure that you are wearing loose, light clothing in a color which feels soothing to you. (Yogi practitioners will usually meditate with little or no clothing.)

So, you are now well located, undisturbed and comfortably dressed with no tight clothing and, at least for now, no jewelry.

Now for your meditation position; The ideal position for meditation is the *lotus* and the reason for this is quite simple. In the lotus position your body is forming a pyramid shape which allows for the optimum flow of energy. Although this is not necessary for you at the beginning, keep it in mind as you may want to develop this position for meditation at a later date. For now, place yourself in that position where you can;

1. Keep the spine straight

2. Remain comfortable for fifteen to twenty minutes without moving

3. Stay awake As you can see, it is possible to meet the conditions above either sitting or lying down.

If you are someone who likes sound around you now is a good time to start playing your favorite meditation music softly in the background. If you like to burn incense it is a good idea to do so about half an hour before you plan to begin your meditation. In that way the scent will not be too strong and cause you to be distracted by your sense of smell.

Once you are comfortably placed begin contact with the Universal Energy. You may like to begin with a prayer such as The Lord's Prayer or the Twenty Third psalm (The Great Invocation), or you may like to choose a mantra like the Aum. Whichever you choose, intone softly and easily.

Now take two or three deep breaths, inhaling slowly and expelling the air from your lungs as fully as possible. Close your eyes, allow your hands to fall naturally on your thighs with first finger and thumb lightly touching and ask for the White Light to flow protectively around you as you meditate.

Now begin the conscious process of relaxation.Start with your toes, first the left foot and then the right, see your toes in your mind and tell them to relax, to let go, order the energy up out of them. Pull the energy up through your body and as you draw it upwards visualize each part of you and command that that part be comfortable and still. Draw the energy up the legs, the hips, the trunk, the hands, the arms. From the base of the spine feel the energy rising up to the back of the neck, each part

3

relaxing as you go. Now relax the scalp, the forehead, the cheeks, the mouth and the throat. You have now relaxed your whole body, which may be feeling heavy and immovable at this time, and you have collected you energy together in one spot. Center this spot behind the forehead, in the area of the *third eye.*

Allow ,now, a troubled mind to become silent. If thoughts and pictures disturb your mind just ignore them, do not give them your attention and they will drift away like clouds on a summers day. You are now at peace with yourself. Be still and know.

If new thoughts and ideas now begin to flow into your mind receive the message they bring and let them go. Do not try to question or understand at this time, just accept the information and release it again. You can *THINK* about that which you received *AFTER* your meditation is over.

If you seem only to draw a blank, don't worry. Some of the most valuable knowledge given to us in meditation does not come to our awareness at the time but will surface later when we have need of such knowledge or when our conscious understanding is ready for it. Just keep in mind that *those who ask receive.*

4

DIAGRAM TO SHOW ENERGY FLOW PATTERN IN THE LOTUS POSITION

At the end of your meditation allow your thoughts to once more focus on the length of your body, returning to it the energy which vitalizes you and notice how refreshed and energized you feel. Remember to give thanks to the Source of Life for your meditation and for the energy which has flown into you. Take a deep breath and know you are calm, at ease and ready to face the world.

This is a standard procedure for meditation and will be referred to as such in the meditations in this book. This standard procedure will take you into the meditative state for your own private meditations as well as those contained here. The contents of this book are outlines of guided meditation paths which you can pursue for enlightenment and help in specific areas of life. The methodology is always the same for going into meditation up to the point where total body relaxation and centering of one's energy is reached after which the *PURPOSE* of the meditation defines the path which is followed.

 THE PURE WHITE LIGHT

We are Children of Light. The Cristos is the Light of Heaven. This pure white light is the positive living energy of the universe from which all good is created. When we wish to sit and contemplate on the spiritual aspects of life, and particularly when we wish to meditate or pray, we should, then, imagine ourselves surrounded by this white light. Imagine that you are on a stage and the spotlight is on you. Now look up and you will see the spotlight comes down around you as a great, circular shaft of white light. When you call the *White Light* of the universe down around you this is what it looks like. If you are not yet able to see it with your eyes, don't worry - if you asked for it, it will be there whether you see it or not! This Light flows endlessly from the Source and by drawing it to us we are erecting a protective shield of positive energy around ourselves and filling our being with strength and energy. This energy brings with it the healing forces, physical, mental and spiritual, of the entire universe

Feel this Light Energy flowing around you and into you through the crown chakra on the top of your head. Know that, as you have asked, it is being directed to you from the Source or from the heart of a highly evolved being. Now you, in turn, can let that energy flow out from your heart, sending love, peace, healing, to all in need and to the planet itself. Send out this energy with humility and compassion and if you wish to direct it to someone in particular, always do so with the added proviso; "*Thy will be done*". This last is to ensure that we do not interfere with anothers' life stream.

Practice calling this energy around you, make it part of you, learn to relax and let go in it's gentle warmth. Aspire to becoming part of that living, loving flow of life yourself

Remember; *We are the Children of Light*.

VISUALIZATION

For this you need a good imagination! You really need to be able to imagine **manifest objects** as they **should be** so start practicing for this type of meditation by looking at a familiar object, say, your watch, and then close your eyes and recreate in your mind's eye every detail of that watch. Keep practicing because one day you may find this a very useful ability, you see, this kind of visualization is the foundation not only of bringing good things into your life, but also of self-healing. In order to heal yourself you must be able to visualize the damaged area in great detail and you must be able to "see" it as perfect. The process for this is as follows;

1. Go into your standard meditation state.

2. Draw the Universal Energy of White Light around you and into you through the crown chakra

3. Mentally direct the flow of energy to that part of the body you need healing

When you are successfully directing the energy you will feel either a tingling sensation in the affected part or a flood of heat which may or may not spread throughout the whole body.

Visualization is also used to manifest in your life those things which you desire to be there. It is an integral part of the projection process. When we project for something we define what it is that we want and we visualize it clearly and precisely and we do this in the meditation state. Once we have completed the projection we release it to the universe and simply wait for it to arrive in our lives. There are two cautions I wish to insert here;

1. Always complete any projection with the words "If this can be done with harm to no one and in accordance with the universal plan"

2. *BE VERY SURE* that you want what you are asking for because you WILL get it. For those of you who have already ceased to want, the best projection which I can offer is a simple statement; "*Let Thy will be my will and let my will be Thy will*".

▲ BALANCING THE CHAKRAS

This is a short meditation which can be undertaken daily in order to maintain good balance and alignment of the chakras. If you are not already familiar with the placement of your energy centers, or chakras, refer to *fig.1*.and for a visualization of this meditation refer first to *fig.2*. It is desirable that you take the lotus position or, failing that, an upright sitting position with bare feet flat on the floor. Take several relaxing breaths and surround yourself, as always, with the *White Light*. Clear your mind of all extraneous thoughts.

Begin now by visualizing the first, or root chakra, and "*see*" it spinning like a wheel in a clockwise direction. As it spins a warm red energy expands outwards from the wheel. *Feel* the warmth of this energy and when you feel it reaching two or three inches in diameter catch a thread of the energy and pull it up to the second chakra. Now, like a child's spinning top, visualize that thread winding around the second chakra and setting it spinning until it rotates at the same rate and with the same energy output as the first. Continue in this same manner up through the seven chakras until all are rotating evenly and in harmony with each other.

Maintain this state for a few minutes and then allow the energy to well up through all seven chakras, out of the crown chakra on the top of your head , arc down on the outside of both arms and resurge up through the soles of your feet. After circulating the energy in this way seven times pull the energy back through the chakras and send it flowing throughout the physical body to energize and revitalize you.

Once you have mastered visualization and control of this energy, refer to *fig. 3*. You will see that this specifies certain colors for each chakra. In the same way that you visualized the red energy for the root chakra you can now practice visualizing the correct energy color for each chakra in turn and visualize the energy arcing from the crown chakra to the feet as either white or rainbow colored. Later, as you become more proficient and confident in your meditations you will find this is a wonderful way to enter upon a spiritual path of astral projection but I do not recommend that you try this at this time if you are a beginner.

THE SEVEN CHAKRAS

<u>Related Glands</u>

Pineal

Thyroid

Thymus

Adrenal

Reproductive

Crown

Third Eye

Throat

Heart

Solar Plexus

Spleen

Root Center

Fig.1.

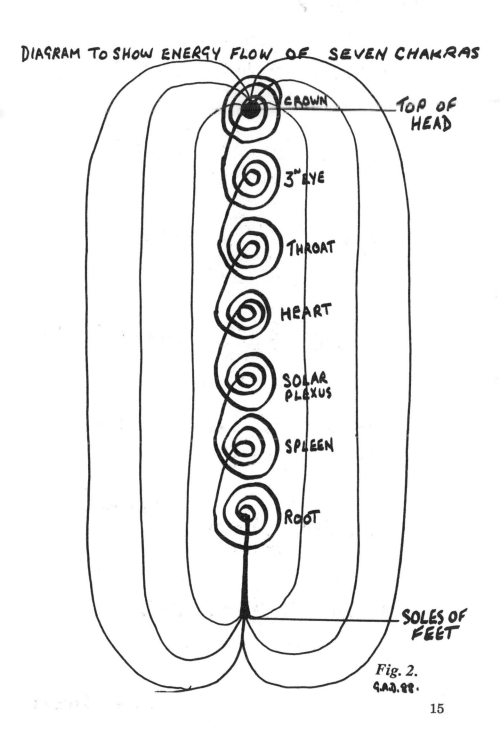

DIAGRAM TO SHOW ENERGY FLOW OF SEVEN CHAKRAS

CROWN — TOP OF HEAD

3ⁿ EYE

THROAT

HEART

SOLAR PLEXUS

SPLEEN

ROOT

SOLES OF FEET

Fig. 2.
G.A.D. 88.

15

TO SHOW COLOR

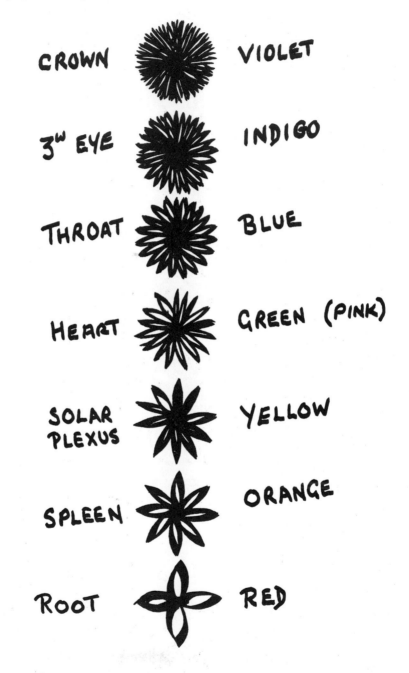

CROWN — VIOLET

3ᵈ EYE — INDIGO

THROAT — BLUE

HEART — GREEN (PINK)

SOLAR PLEXUS — YELLOW

SPLEEN — ORANGE

ROOT — RED

Fig. 3.   GAD.88

THE STRESS FACTOR

Perhaps one of the most useful aspects of meditation for the busy person today is the way in which it can relieve stress. It has been shown to me that it is not necessarily overwork, deadlines to be met or problematic situations in life which cause stress. In fact there are many happy and relaxed people who thrive under great pressure and only become "stressed" when they are bored and have nothing to do. So, what *REALLY* causes the stress in your life? I am told, by my guides, that it is *FEAR* which causes stress. And that makes a lot of sense. It is not the *DEADLINE* but fear of failure to meet it which stresses you. It is not the amount of work you have to do but fear that the Boss will not be satisfied that stresses you, and so on. This particular meditation is, then, designed to relieve stress not only in a particular situation which you may be going through but in all areas of your life. It is more to teach you how to prevent stress rather than allow it to build and then have to be relieved.

For this meditation the breathing exercises are very important so begin in this way;

1. Stand with legs slightly apart and hands clasped with fingers interlaced down in front of you.

2. Take a deep breath in and as you do so slowly raise your arms, fingers still linked, up over your head. Pause there for a moment and then unlock the fingers and bring the arms out to the sides at full stretch and down to the starting position, exhaling fully and slowly as you do so. Repeat this three times.

3. Take two or three light, normal breaths.

4. Breathe in deeply and, bending slightly forward and with hands on knees, exhale as hard as you can. Do this once only.

5. Now lie down (or take the lotus position) and begin the standard relaxation process.

6. You now have your consciousness focused in the area of the third eye. *DO NOT* project outward this time. Instead turn your attention inward.

Allow your *Spiritual Self* to view your *Physical Self* objectively, as if your physical self were a separate person.

When you look at "Joe" you will be aware in an uncritical way of all that "Joe" is afraid of, you will pass no judgment on this awareness, but only register it as part of the reality of "Joe".

This is as far as you may wish to go with this meditation the first time and I suggest that you wait two or three days before continuing.

Going into this meditation again use the same process as before. This time of course you are already aware of "Joe's" fears so we may proceed from where the last effort left off. First choose one of the least troublesome of "Joe's" fears and set it aside (I will tell you why later). Now you can take the fears one by one and deal with them by understanding and compassion for "Joe". Realize that your stress stems from fears which are grounded in the physical world and that world at best is impermanent. *Know that in any given situation you can only ever do your best in the light of the knowledge you have.* Now look at the stress pattern due to fear of failure to meet a deadline. Ask yourself what is the worst that can happen it you fail, "Will the world come to an end?" *No,*
"Will I die?" *No,*
"Will my nearest and dearest be lost to me?" *No.*

"Is the deadline reasonable for the work to be done?". If it is not then you only need to do your best. If it is reasonable but you are sure you cannot meet it then you have to begin a whole new examination of your true capabilities in light of your new self awareness.

Do you see how this works for you? It allows you to look in a non-judgmental way at the way you, "Joe", operate in your daily life and through this wholesome and uncluttered awareness of yourself you can shed your fears and thereby avoid stress.

Earlier I asked you to mentally set aside one of "Joe's" less troublesome stress causing problems. Now I will explain why. The body is a strange mechanism and most bodies actually enjoy being stressed or worrying about something. Have you watched children playing and seen how they love to give themselves a fright? It seems that the body gets some vicarious pleasure out of fear and therefore I have found that you will find it easier to let go of the fears which are restricting you and causing you stress if you allow yourself the indulgence of one specific fear. Indulge your body in a fear of snakes or flying or something which will not interfere with your daily life. Further, allow yourself that indulgence in a specifically controlled way for example, tell "Joe" he is allowed to be stressed about and fear flying every Friday from noon to ten pm. That way you can fly anywhere without stress at anytime except Fridays and by pouring all your stress energy into the "Friday Flying Fear" you will keep your body "Stress Happy" and not need to waste energy fearing other things which were causing stress in your life. This technique may sound rather silly but experience has shown me that it works very well for many people. As I believe stress is the reason for many of the ills to which we succumb in life I decided to include this meditation technique on the basis that if you are stressed, then it is well worth a try.

WEIGHT CONTROL

There is really only one way to control weight in a normally healthy person and that is to control eating. Accepting that you wish to stay in good shape first you must find which is the right weight for you. If you already overweight you need to know why. To find the answer to either of these questions you can go into the standard meditation state, once you are totally relaxed with the energy centered in the third eye follow these steps;

1. Allow your consciousness to formulate the question, " Why am I overweight at this time". The answer to this is certainly stored in your Higher Consciousness and may relate to a present problem or a past life situation, for example, many people with a weight problem today experienced severe hunger in a previous life. Once the answer is given to you come out of the meditation and think about the answer you received for a few days.

2. You are now fully aware of the cause of your problem and need to know the correct weight for you in this lifetime. Again go into your meditative state and project the question to your Higher Self. The answer to this question will often come to you as a visual picture

of how you should look and you may also hear, or see, a specific number related to your weight. Do not be surprised if the size you are told is right for you is more or less than the standard charts you are used to looking at, remember, those charts arc a guide for everyone but the information you receive is personal to you alone. One other thing to keep in mind, although ascetics favor the lean and hungry look, in reality spiritual learning and growth takes a lot of physical energy so if you are truly a student of metaphysics you may be shown a weight level several pounds more than you would wish as being the right size for you at this time.

Once you have identified both the cause of any weight problem you may have and found the right weight for you then you can add a visualization meditation in which you will "see" yourself exactly as you should be. This visualization will greatly assist any dietary control you are undertaking, whether to gain or to lose weight.

SMOKING

As with weight control, you need first to identify why you smoke and then make a decision to stop, assuming that is what you wish to do. The same kind of procedure as with weight control applies here and your visualisation will include "seeing" yourself with clean healthy lung and undertaking such activities as running and playing energetic games.

If you are not an habitual smoker you can probably stop at will but if you are a long standing user of tobbacco you may find playing one of the self hypnosis "stop smoking" tapes will help you as you meditate.Ultimately, as with any habit, you have to want to break it if you are to have a lasting success.

8 PROBLEM SOLVING

Whether the problem you are dealing with is personal or work related the method of finding the answer is the same. Let us say for example that you are designing a new home and you want to add a sewing room but the present plans do not seem to allow any space for you to do so. In your meditation visualize the plan as it exists and then, separately visualize the sewing room you wish to add into the plan. Imagine the drawing for the sewing room floating freely over the top of the main plan, go over all the existing dimensions in your mind and then ask that you be shown how you may best include the sewing room into the plan. Remain quiet and relaxed for a few more minutes allowing the whole matter to drift away from you and then go about your regular business, forgetting all about the sewing room. It may take a day or two for the results you are seeking but be sure you will receive an answer to the problem in one way or an another. Maybe your architect, or a member of the family will "suddenly come up with a bright idea" or maybe you yourself will find the answer coming to you. It doesn't matter how the answer comes, only that you receive it, and this you will surely do. It's worth mentioning here that if you are the one to receive the answer to the problem then you may have had a combination of things at work for you; one, through your meditation you released the problem to the universal mind and so were open to "outside" help. Two, you opened your mind to input from your own Higher Consciousness and three, you programmed your physical brain to run a search of all your previously stored information and possible answers for you. The source of the answer received is somewhat irrelevant if the problem is satisfactorily resolved.

THE RIVER CROSSING

This meditation will do two things for you. One, it will show you those problems for which you are expected to find solution and two, it will refresh body and soul with universal energy. I hope that you will enjoy it as I do.

Before we begin this meditation I would like to tell you about the symbolic meanings it contains. Our journey takes us first down a straight narrow pathway. This path is the road to inner peace. On either side of the path are tall pine trees; Pines have a special healing, cleansing quality all their own. As we walk along the path the trunks of the trees blot out all that is going on around us and the branches arch over our heads, sending down their soothing energies. At the end of the path we come to a river of crystal clear flowing water. We cross through the water and as we do so we cleanse our minds and our bodies. On the far side of the river we turn to face the river. Taking our problems, one by one, we cast them into the flowing stream. If the river carries them away from us we need not concern ourselves with those problems as they will find their own solution, but those problems which rise to the surface at our feet are our rightful responsibility and we must take them back to ourselves and look for their solution within us. Imagine, if you will, that you are a small child. your toy is broken and your shoelace undone. You go to your father for help. Might he not say to you "let me have your toy and I will fix it for you, but you are a big boy now so sit down and tie your own shoelace"? So it is with our problems. Sometimes the lesson is to learn to solve the problem ourself. So, an important benefit of this meditation is that it helps you to see which difficulties you are meant to resolve for yourself and which you will have help with.

Now that we know which of our problems we must deal with, let us continue our journey in search of answers.

Turning our back once more on the river we will go forward towards a brightly lit open space. In the center you will see a table and on the table a silver cup.

The cup is forever being filled with a stream of sparkling, living, flowing energy from above. Drink from this cup and feel the energy flowing through you, reaching every cell of your body, making it perfect and whole. As the energy flows through you become aware of the lightness of your body and open your being to the enlightenment of higher consciousness. Allow yourself to blend with the universal soul wherein all things are known.

Now we will return to the point of our beginning in this meditation.

One thing more I would like to share with you about this, or any other meditation; I am sure you have heard the scientists say that we normally use only about ten percent of our brain and that ninety percent lies dormant, untapped. In much the same way I believe that only a very small part of our eternal intellect accompanies us into each incarnation and that, in meditation, we are creating the link between our earthly and heavenly intellect. We are learning to draw from our own deep well of greater knowledge and wisdom. In this meditation we symbolically do this when we drink from the silver cup. Although there will be times when you need to appeal to a higher authority for help, once you have mastered this meditation you will be surprised at the depth of your own soul's knowledge and wisdom.

THE SEVEN RAYS

The White Light is the culmination of all the colors and is at the core of each ray of the spectrum. The individual rays may be drawn in during meditation to help in the specific areas which are listed below. When you wish to draw in these rays I have found the most effective way is to lie down flat on your back with the arms folded across the chest and the ankles crossed. In this position go through your relaxation and White Light process and then visualize the particular ray you need as a bright beam of the correct color descending down directly into the chakra with which that color is associated, for example; draw the red ray down into the root chakra for an increase in physical energy.

The Violet Ray is one which can be used to very good effect on a daily basis because it enables you to transmute you karma, something which is necessary and beneficial to all of us who are endeavoring to make progress. To help with your visualization see *fig.4*. The transmutation of karma through this meditation means that your karma may be set aside to be dealt with at a better time or in a different way than you are now experiencing.

The Green Ray is directed to the heart and opens us to a true understanding of compassion and unconditional love. It is also the ray of healing.

RED RAY FOR PHYSICAL ENERGY

ORANGE RAY FOR BALANCE OF PHYSICAL LOVE

YELLOW RAY FOR PHILOSOPHICAL AWARENESS

GREEN RAY FOR COMPASSION

BLUE RAY FOR SPIRITUAL AWARENESS; GUIDE COMMUNICATION;

INDIGO RAY FOR ALTERED PERCEPTIONS

VIOLET RAY FOR TRANSMUTATION OF KARMA

These rays can, of course, be directed towards other people by you but before you do this be sure that you are not going to interfere with their life's stream as this is not

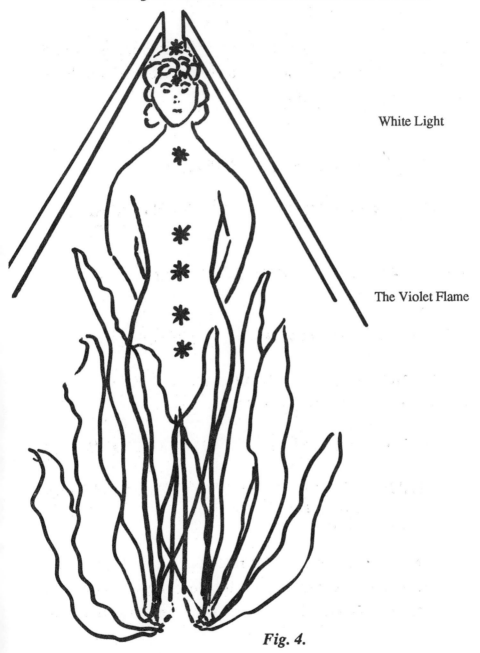

White Light

The Violet Flame

Fig. 4.

permissible; also know that if you do direct energy in this way to another person you are accepting responsibility for the results: this is one way in which Karmic ties are created for the future, so be careful.

▲ PAST LIVES

Looking at past lives can be both fun and informative. The serious student of metaphysics who is looking for spiritual growth will understand that by recalling past life situations we can acquire many clues as to the reason for this lifetime and the things we need to learn. Past life recall may also give us greater understanding of the actual physical and emotional problems being faced in this life, as not all difficulties arise in the life being lived currently but often stem from past events. If that sounds unlikely think of how modern psychiatry so often dates adult problems back to your childhood experiences. We are just taking that idea one step further and relating to past life experiences. For example, let us say that a past life shows you living in a miserable, cold and damp environment and that you died at an early age and extremely angry with your lot. Now in this lifetime you are plagued with a rheumatic condition. This present condition could be a carry over from that past life; not because of the cold and damp, but because you have not let go of the anger you felt previously.Obviously not all your present ailments relate to the past as clearly as this example, but if you can find the source of your complaint you are well on the way to doing something about it, and isn't that true of all things -- *"find the cause and you are on the way to the cure"*? We might also keep in mind that at the root of everything is the inescapable truth that we are the cause of all that happens to us; We reap as we have sown. So you can see how looking at the situations in our past could well help us to deal more effectively with our present and so create for ourselves a better future.

How to do this through meditation:

You will of course begin in the usual way by surrounding yourself with the white light of goodness and protection, next you will go through your regular relaxation technique and bring yourself to the third eye point of focus. Now use this invocation; *"I ask that I may be given access to my own Akashic record and that, with the help of my spiritual guides and protectors, I may be shown that which I need to know from my past to better help me relate to the present and for the benefit of my soul's growth"*.

At this point state that you only wish to be an observer of the past and that you do not wish to relive the experience. This is very important as reliving an unpleasant past life experience may prove extremely traumatic.

Next visualize yourself climbing aboard some conveyance to your liking and command the driver, not to go forwards, but to go backwards, backwards until you reach a point of reference your guides feel it will be useful for you to observe.

Once your vehicle stops look out of the window and observe all that you are being shown.

At the first visit to a particular place and time there will usually be no action, no sound, just a scene to be viewed. If this is the case, once you have the scene firmly fixed in your mind, order your driver to return you home and come out of the meditation as usual.

The next time you go on this meditation trip your starting point is the visualization of the scene you were shown before. Once you are yet again at that place and time you may ask your guides for more information about the scene and then the events that took place there will unfold before you. It may be a dreary situation or it may be an epic on the grand scale, but whatever it is you can be sure there is a lesson there for you which is very relevant to your present life.

As a general rule it is as well to stick to one past life until you have understood it's meaning for you in this life before you start tracking down other previous lives, but some people have a knack for this type of meditation and once they start the old lives come flooding into memory, sometimes even without going into the meditative state. After all, you are not asking to be shown new things, you are simply asking to recall that which is lost to present memory.

If you use this meditation wisely it can help you to add considerable worth to your present life experience, but do be cautioned against using it as an escape or you could just use up your time watching old movies and learning nothing.

⚠️ACCESSING YOUR HIGHER CONSCIOUSNESS

One of the objectives of meditation is to put us in contact with our Higher Consciousness, to enable us to tap into the reservoir of our greater knowledge and awareness. But first, what do I mean when I say Higher Consciousness? To me it is that part of ourselves which has remained on the immortal plane during our present incarnation. Are you familiar with those children's balloons which are long sausage-like things and you can twist little pieces of them into small bubbly knobs? Sometimes I think of the soul, the total consciousness that is "*me*", as one of these balloons. In any given lifetime the amount of "*soul awareness*" that I need to fulfill that life's tasks is like one of those bubbly knobs, segregated from the whole to accompany me to earth but never completely cut off. When doing this meditation I am re-opening the doorway to that larger self and so giving access to the knowledge and understanding of many previous lives. Do not be deceived into thinking that your Higher Consciousness knows everything and cannot be wrong. *It can only make available to you that which you have already learned in the past*, but if you learned well there is much for you to draw upon. Just keep in mind that, although your Higher self is incapable of deliberately misleading you, it may be perpetrating a previous misunderstanding and can only present information to you in as far as it's own growth and development allow. It, like you, is in a process of growth and is only the culmination of your own previous experience.

(I would just like to add a note here for purpose of clarification that the soul and the soul essence are seen by me as two integral, but separable, things.)

For this meditation I suggest that you use some visualization and you might like to try it in this way;

Sit comfortably in a chair, undisturbed and alone. Place your feet flat on the floor and open your hands, palms up, on your lap.

Close your eyes lightly and run quickly through your relaxation technique, bringing the White Light down and around you.

Do all this carefully but as quickly as possible. The reason I suggest you do it quickly and with the minimum of fuss is because, unlike when you are communicating with much higher beings, this process of communicating with yourself should be, I feel, treated as a more every day matter so that you may be comfortable and at ease with the idea.

So, you are now ready to begin the meditation proper. Concentrate on that center of energy behind the third eye which is "you" in this life.

Now imagine a thread like a telephone wire connecting the present "*you*" to all the past "*yous*". If you wish you can actually imagine picking up a telephone and dialing to your other self, although I prefer to think of a small door opening in the top of the head. Just open that door and call through to request the information you need. Your Higher Consciousness can always be counted on to bring to your attention the best possible experiential advice and so help you with the vast majority of problems you have to deal with. So long as you remember that even your Higher Consciousness does not know everything I feel this meditation is well worth your attention.

There are those who feel that one should always appeal to much Higher Authority and, while I do not disagree with that, I think we should try to understand our lives through our own efforts as far as possible. After all, you don't learn too much if someone tells you all the answers do you? and you will be surprised at just how much you really do know if you master this meditation and open up those lines of communication between you and you.

# ENLIGHTENMENT

Meditation for the purpose of enlightenment is perhaps the most difficult but is almost always the most rewarding. When the enlightenment we seek pertains to a mundane matter we must be prepared to be shown ourselves as we truly are. So often in a difficult situation we see the "other party" as in the wrong and behaving badly but when we meditate and ask for enlightenment we may be in for a few surprises. Our own sweet nature and generous outlook may seem a whole lot less desirable and more manipulative than we imagined! So be prepared for some shocks!

The consolation is that as you learn and grow one of the great lessons you are taught is acceptance, and that includes acceptance of yourself, warts and all.

When you seek spiritual enlightenment and direct your meditation to your Teachers on the higher planes you should be willing to prepare properly for such a meditation. Such preparation might follow this path;

Prior to the meditation period avoid eating red meat and heavy foods; eat lightly.

Be sure you and your clothing is fresh and clean.

Go to the meditation calmly, do not go with anger towards anyone in your mind.

Take extra time with the breathing and relaxation process. When all your energy is well centered behind the third eye allow it to rest there for a few moments.

Now project your energy forward for about a foot in front of you.

Be silent and still within yourself.

First there will be blackness before you and then a widening purplish blue hole will appear and expand to fill the blackness.

Next the hole will fill with light and into this light will come enlightenment.

You may hear sounds, words, or you may be shown writing or pictures.

Whichever the way your guides are choosing to teach you, the message you receive will have profound meaning for you. But remember that it is FOR YOU so keep it to yourself. As a general rule a student of metaphysics should share their meditations only with their teachers, so, in your meditations question all that your earthly teacher is telling you and question your earthly teacher about your meditations.

The search for enlightenment is the search for Truth after which we are all seekers.

⚠ A CHRISTMAS MEDITATION

This guided Christmas meditation was channeled to me for our group meditation at our Christmas gathering in 1987. During this meditation we played the chakra balancing tape which the group had put together during our last series of classes. The tape is one comprising of single chord resonances, each of five minutes duration, which we found to be most effective for balancing the chakras. Should you wish, a copy of this tape may be obtained from me or you can try this meditation with any appropriate chakra balancing tape which you already have. If you are doing this meditation as a group, which is the way we were doing it, you might care to sit round in a circle and join hands.

Begin by bringing the white light down and around you, take two or three relaxing breaths and then follow the flow of energy up through the chakras with the visualization as follows;

Root chakra; *"The night is dark. A cold wind is blowing over the stony desert. Look to the west. High in the night sky a brilliant new star is shining. The caravan you are* with moves out with bells ringing softly on the pack animals as you head towards the west".

Second chakra; "*The journey is long and hard. You must gather all your resources to go on. Let go of all that is slowing you down. So long as the star shines to guide you you are determined to go on*".

Third chakra; "*A new day is breaking. You are approaching a town and the star has paled in the light of day. You seek out the king and ask "where is the newborn heir to the kingdom?". The king sends you to seek out this child and when evening comes you see again the star. It shines over Bethlehem.*

Fourth chakra; "*What joy! The child is found. As you gather round you marvel at the bright aura of Truth and Love. You feel the energy of everlasting life flowing from this tiny child to you and you make your offering of devotion*".

Fifth chakra; "*From this day it becomes your vow that no wrong words will leave your mouth. That all your words will speak the love and joy of life*".

Sixth chakra; *"Turn now to face the East. You begin the journey home. As you travel over the desert once again you turn your mind inward, allowing all that you have seen to wash over you, he absorbed by you, be understood".*

Seventh chakra; *"You are home. The Truth is in you and of you. The energy of life flows into your crown chakra; A giant arch of silver light spanning two thousand years".*

You, Christ, You.

GUIDE COMMUNICATION

These instructions were received by me in February of this year, 1988, from my spiritual guide, David. As I followed the instructions and produced excellent results you may like to try the same process for yourself. I was told to place certain crystals around me and sit in silent meditation, thus allowing my guide to enhance the vibratory field and increase the ease of communication between us. The effect was quite noticeable to me and I decided to share the experience with my class members;

This is what we did;

1. Sit in the lotus position to create the energy pyramid

2. Go through the standard relaxation procedure

3. Balance the chakras until all are in harmonic motion

4. State that you wish to better open your channels of communication with your guide and you therefore give your permission for the guides to work on your energy field.

5. Ask that your spiritual guide show you

    a. The direction you should face (North, South etc)
    b. The stones or crystals you should use
    c. The placement of the stones or crystals

Once you are given the information try to sit in silent meditation with the stones or crystals given for about ten minutes every few days. Remember the old rule that all spiritual experience is transferred to the physical body, so make haste slowly and enjoy the widening of your awareness.

YOUR SECRET NAME

Following shortly after the "Guide Communication" instructions it was shown to me that it is possible to find your "real" or secret name. This is the vibratory tone to which you, and you alone, have vibrated since your sentient self came into existence. As it is the VIBRATION which is being sought, it may be given to you as a word, name or just as a sound, but whichever it is it belongs to you exclusively and you should keep it to yourself. Can you see the necessity for this secrecy? Knowing the tone of your personal vibration, the frequency which reaches the deepest part of you, could be a dangerous tool in the wrong hands, so please, tell no one.

Once you have your "*name*" one of the best ways to use it is as an intonation during your meditations, it seems to work most effectively when used in combination with the universal Aum to create a balanced energy field around you at the point where you have gone into relaxation and centered your energy in the area of the third eye. I believe that in addition to a better balanced field you will also experience greater receptivity and clarity during the remainder of your meditation.

And now, the means of acquiring your "*name*";

The steps are virtually the same as those for your crystals and stones, ie;

1. Sit in the lotus position

2. Relaxation procedure

3. Balance the chakras and once they are all in harmonic motion be conscious of reaching up through the crown chakra with your energy.

4. Ask your spiritual guide to help you access your own akashic record and become aware of your original vibration.

5. Carefully note the *Sound and Intonation* of your vibration, repeat it aloud to be sure you have it correctly.

As a note to the above I wish to add this; It may be that you will first be given names from past lives where there are karmic ties to this life and lessons still to be learned before you are ready to receive your "*true*" vibration so I suggest that, having once received a "*name*", you ask your guide to show you if this has any past life associations for you to learn from and what they may be.

Can you imagine the famous opening to Beethoven's Fifth without the fourth note? Your "*name*", your "*Vibration*", is an equally important part of the symphony of humanity without which the whole concert of life would be diminished, so guard it well.

▲RAINBOW MEDITATION

This last meditation was channeled by Laura Parrett, a member of our study group. Most of Laura's work with spirit is in the realm of herbs and healing and this, the Rainbow meditation, was designated for healing and balancing. We hope that you enjoy working using it in your search for balance and harmony.

As you relax, picture yourself being wrapped in a white light. The Christ White Light. You are warm and safe and comfortable. As you inhale, you bring that white light through the crown of your head. Bring it down to your spine to your heart, then to the solar plexus. Now the light is down to the spleen in the navel area, then to the base of your spine.

As you exhale, you loosen the tension and debris held within. You may now be rid of it.

Inhale white light, exhale, letting go, letting go.

Now imagine a rainbow of beautiful colors in the white light above and around you.

The first color is a beautiful clear red. The red ray is coming down to the base of your spine. The color is warm and healing the pelvic area. Balancing the energy through your base energy center.

The second color is clear orange. The orange ray is entering the naval area and the spleen. It's warm, healing energy is allowing the body to rid it's toxic waste and balance your splenic energy center.

The third color coming down is the beautiful golden yellow of the sun. This yellow is entering the solar plexus. Felling the warm, healing sun energy throughout your solar plexus, allowing emotional release and balancing this energy center within.

The fourth ray coming down is a brilliant green. This is entering your heart. this warm and healing energy of the green ray is opening and balancing your heart energy center and allowing universal love and forgiveness to enter.

The fifth ray is the blue of the sky. It is clear and beautiful entering your throat center. You feel the warmth and healing as the blue ray balances the energies and allows your thoughts to come through.

The next ray is a beautiful indigo. As the indigo ray enters the brow area you feel peace. This ray is balancing the brow energy center and allowing your higher self, your higher consciousness to be recognized.

The next ray is violet and is entering the energy center at the crown of your head. The violet is balancing and healing your spiritual nature.

Now as all the colors of the rainbow have entered your body and all the energy centers, they all become the protective white light energy, passing through all parts of your body, you feel relaxed and tranquil. You may now wake up and feel refreshed and well.

AMEN

JOANNE HEINZ
P.O. Box 411
Ravenna, Ohio 44266

The Author

Gillian DeArmond Came to the United States from England in 1981. She worked for many years as a registered nurse in England, Scotland and Indonesia but was always involved in metaphysics. She was the pupil of Edna Maye, a well known Yorkshire clairvoyant, and while in Indonesia studied the Buddhist philosophy with Tjoa Joe Seng as well as Chinese numerology, the Tarot and Astrology. Gillian currently lives in Plymouth, Michigan where she teaches metaphysics and gives personal life readings.